A

STRATEGY

OF

MIRRORS

A
STRATEGY
OF
MIRRORS

Derek J Brown

with an introduction
by Peter Clive

First published 2020
by Rymour Books
45 Needless Road
PERTH
EH2 0LE

© Derek J Brown 2020

ISBN 978-1-8381863-1-9

Cover design by Ian Spring
Typeset in Garamond
Printed and bound by
Imprint Digital
Seychelles Farm
Upton Pyne
Exeter

The paper used in this book is approved
by the Forest Stewardship Council

CONTENTS

Acknowledgements	8
Introduction	9
George Square	11
Calcolo Di Una Dea	15
Old Man in the Museum	17
Blue Angel on Union Street	19
City Built on the Holy Ground of Contradiction	21
Like a Marcel Duchamp Painting	23
Because	25
Cosmic Salt on an Earthly Wound	26
Equivalent of a Blank Piece of Paper	27
City in Mist: 6.27AM	29
Winter Rain	30
Red and Yellow	32
Central Station	34
The Universe Has Countless Houses	36
Torch Song	38
A State of Not Knowing	40
Messiah	42
Stranger on Probation	44
The Day Gene Vincent Came to Glasgow	46
One Day Everything Will Melt	48
Gypsy Girl With Mandolin	50
Antithesis of Everything	52
Abstract Curtains	53
Alexander Hutchinson	55
The Glass Harmonica	57

Random Number Generator 58

Dyslexic Birds in Olympic Dullness 60

Nabokovian 61

Anathema 62

Nonchalant Fixation on a Naked Ballerina 64

The Mythology of Progress 66

Gospel of the Notes and Keys 68

Buddha Unbecoming 70

In Memory of the Present 72

Image of You Descending 74

Courses Echoes Take 76

The Barbarity of Glass 78

The Seagulls of Sauchiehall Street 80

The Head of a Pin 83

Below a Moon of Soft Suspense 84

Beyond the Sense of Ashes 85

Inpenetrable Whispers of a Thin-skinned Nude 86

Physicality of Water 88

Order of the Locusts 89

The Aletheia Within You 90

Senile Woman in the Corner 91

The Very First Days of February 92

City Chambers Masquerade 93

Another Attempt at a Love Poem 95

Particles and Waves 96

Sleeping Man on a Red Couch 97

Lady With the Broken Laptop 99

Of Memory 101

Windows 102

Sound of a Subway Train Heading East 103

7

Everything is Paradox	105
Saturnalia of Chaos	106
Physiology is Strange	108
Love is Just a Sundog…	109
Glissando	110
Blue Infinity on Main Street	111
Syllables	113
Everything is Sad This Morning	114
Antipathy of Lamps	115
The Flesh of Memory	116
Tinkling Cymbals	118
Fractals of the Cathkin Braes	120
Two Lovers Lost in a Train Compartment	122
City Fragment Thru a Fractured Lens	123
Statue of an Armless Woman	126
One Man Caught in a Multitude of Self	129
Ashtray Blues	132
St Andrew's Bridge	134
Ten Swords	136

ACKNOWLEDGEMENTS

With grateful thanks to (in no particular order): Ian Spring, Ruby McCann, Iain (Smiddy) Smith, Nigel Chilton, Clare McGrory, Danny Lafferty, Margaret and Bill Shannon, Kyle Holland for the back cover photo, , the Jewish guy in the hoodie whom I met back in 1991, the guy I encountered one day in Rutherglen Main Street who looked like Buddha, the taxi driver obsessed with encyclopædias, the stranger on the late night bus who told me he was from another planet and all the rest…

Derek J Brown 2020

INTRODUCTION

In *A Strategy of Mirrors* Derek Brown has given us 'an intangible / glimpse of what might have been Atlantis'. He describes a 'City Built on The Holy Ground of Contradiction,' his mirrors drawing us into a world populated by 'people that have never heard the sound of their own voices'. Themes of estrangement and alienation are manifested through the false oppositions of our world of 'fool-proof imperfections,' contradictions that create the space in which we imagine ourselves.

This is a work of glorious 'meteoric residues,' relics that have fallen to an undeserving Earth to linger and radiate heat as poetry. There is a sense of being out of place that enables the poet to interrogate that place, a sense of place created by displacement. We are taken through a city where the 'world itself seems drawn / by an inconsistent hand,' where 'screams of doves equate / to the language of the insects,' and where reason is inadequate, there is no explanation accessible to language unless one uses poetry to pass beyond the veil of words to which we are heir, 'because / there is no because'.

'Ever since God turned my ankles I have limped'. This line made me think of Robert Graves's insight—the poet as holy cripple, and Brown's poems take us on an Orphic pilgrimage through a city, not of dreadful night, but dreadful day, for it is filled with an unforgiving sunlight that occupies the space between the mirrors of the title.

The crippling nature of poetry, of grinding meaning from contradiction, on passing through the veil of language to conjure reality from the void, of summoning fire from the long dead embers that are the words we inherit, to describe worlds that can't be understood, leaves us a frustrated Orpheus of modernity trapped 'between the crowded heart and remotest mind' in a circular pilgrimage above ground in a place more mysterious than any in the underworld, and one from which there is no escape, one in which 'truth must oscillate,' and his uninterested Eurydice, 'the blonde woman with sunglasses,' confirms that 'there is nothing here to romanticize, no hell to imparadise'. So, we are left with life flashing before the eyes of 'an invisible, practical mind dying slowly of metaphor'. 'This is the tyranny of atoms. This is the laughter of the sphinx'.

This collection expresses exactly the kind of vision I seek in the poetry I read, an understanding acquired past the limits of exhaustion, a knowledge that turns metaphysics into a childish toy. In an age in which pestilence have taken away our naïve assumptions, this collection belongs in the space they have vacated.

Peter Clive, 2020

GEORGE SQUARE

I

Buchanan Street: God strums a cheap guitar
Discording notes and clashing chords
The primitive civilised

From the city square I sense
false profits,
zigzag philosophies
Familiar falls mysterious
Men utter reds, women yellows,
shadows of gallantry, romance
that's not romance,
heavens monotone, depths lilting
From the memory of music to the music of memory

architecture floats (countless eyes of one)
inside of which
right becomes left
and left becomes right
A lack of structure itself a structure

On a wooden bench
sits an old woman in black furs,
she looks like a time traveller
engaged in a kind of conversation (in a silent way)
with nothing in particular,
in tune with not being in tune
She looks like she knows it is not enough to know

A STRATEGY OF MIRRORS

 A fat man eats a peach, down his chin the juice descends,
a young couple fake an old school nervosa,
dream opposites and valentines
The old pass without knowing they are old
Falter the coffee cup minds,
rebounds a fog of saxophone,
from rejection as acceptance to acceptance as rejection

All around I hear
a churning of things divided by the fact they are the same,
minds that mimic movies,
people that have never heard their own voices

I feel like taking a train to somewhere,
anywhere

II

From pale white bodies red flowers blossom,
men dressed as women pose as shamans,
ritual clowns eat excrement

Ever since God turned my ankles I have limped,
passing a young man repeatedly
throwing Finnegan's Wake at a wall,
call me Hermes as I walk unnoticed,
through a myriad of arches
emblazoned with words such as liberty

Far past these art deco fantasies, these irresistible acidities,
these shadow Juliets, clown-face Romeos,

pieces of a truth must oscillate
Some claim to believe in nothing
and yet there is no such thing as a nihilist
In all this metropolitan mysticism
anyone can find something to love
Between the crowded heart and remotest mind
the tangible must move

Middle aged upper middle-class women
flutter their new eyelashes
and fantasize about Charles Rennie Mackintosh
Within, all is cenotaphic,
and we who count these hours and days
shall end in mistranslated time

There are varying degrees of greatness to fakeness,
meteoric residues, crevasses that rise
There is shadowed flesh, sun-burst bone
There are things that go unmirrored,

bogus policemen that bumble to and fro,
cosmic offices, their windows aslant,
traffic that never starts or stops,
museums that house the indefinable
Faint traces of the pre twenty-first century naked

All you that conquered death, arise
There flourishes a faintness, talk of a subsection,
an unknowable subsidiary
Instruments instrumental in worlds without instruments

III

A STRATEGY OF MIRRORS

I see the day when everything appears motionless
as a sheet over a face that is dead,
as a locked iron gate to a terribly large mansion,
as a frozen train track in a Russian winter,
as a broken clock on the face of a tower

But when you look at it, nothing is motionless
This is the tyranny of atoms. This is the laughter of
  the sphinx

CALCOLO DI UNA DEA

You take my side, drive your sword on through it
I give you my praise and offer you the other
It is true that I am mortal, but so is everyone,
everyone except you, your glittering aloneness
dissevers, reconstructs me, a simulation among many

Demarcating secret of sea and tide and wave
you rise from the foam, taking care not to
incite war you unveil your freak humility
You know I am no threat, I gather all my scars
I place them at your feet, you smile, you laugh

In rayless consummation I am not quite kneeling,
but almost, my back to moon and stars and death
arranged as something else, but not life, not life,
something far more lucid, an infinite facsimile
Unprepared to worship I worship all the same

that which now resembles you more than you yourself,
that's ready to cure disease but just as ready to instil it,
an explosion of conspiracy the undigested truth
All your followers have unfollowed you
and now they follow nothing, not even themselves

For them you have no pity, they mimic savage dogs,
sell their latent souls for scraps of recognition
You speak of the hunter, he who soon must come,
with his eyes closed to his own bloodstained end

A STRATEGY OF MIRRORS

You speak of cruel, inhuman, subtlety of justice,

of the imprecise yet true anguish of false labour,
of a sacred law once broken stays forever broken
You speak of the numberless and their numbers,
heroes to entrap and cowards to protect
Whom will you enlist to exact your strange revenge?

OLD MAN IN THE MUSEUM

Old man in the museum
stops at nothing,
not at the abstract
masquerading as concrete,
not at the sculptures
that invert what is human,
not at the vanities,
nor the lack of them

He dismisses soft fusions
of stone and glass,
hybrid mentalities,
what he prays is a dream,
flesh automatons,
mechanical souls,
lucid machinery
of cartilage and bone

He passes the child
caressing the sarcophagus,
its crimeless eyes wishing
they could see inside of it
He passes the tourists
in their search of a culture,
one that he knows

may not have existed. At last,
the old man stops,
Dali's Saint John of the Cross

DEREK J BROWN

A STRATEGY OF MIRRORS

sensuously transmitting
its coherent mystery,
he cries, almost silently,
though many can hear him,
he cries, not to elicit sympathy,
but to defy it, an invisible,
practical mind dying,
slowly of metaphor

BLUE ANGEL ON UNION STREET

Out of all the blue angels
on Union Street
he was the bluest,
with his blue face
and his blue eyes
and his blue mouth
and his blue hands
and his blue clothes

As if he had stepped
straight out of the bible
he stared into me
and through me,
his blue eyes unredeeming
the redeemed
And the cars that passed
were not really there
and the clouds that passed
were not really there,
only unwieldy dimensions,
foolproof imperfections

More than just sincere
he whispered in my ear
hints of unusual wisdom,

muses killed by sunlight,
evil-minded handmaidens,

April's disfigured shadows,
May's slowly dying warriors,
fugitive loves of June,
gaudy meteors of July,
strange entities of August,
September's new machines
and all that must come after,
what surely
must come after

Out of all the blue angels
on Union Street
he was
undoubtedly
the bluest

CITY BUILT ON THE HOLY GROUND
OF CONTRADICTION

You were a sympathy card unsent,
a predetermined accident,
a body not yet dissected,
a simulation reselected,
a denial now denied,
a dream we were alive,
a frozen meditation,
a myth of separation,
a mask that mourns
its vanished face,
a delegate of a dying race,
a sultan of heat soliciting ice,
a discounted sacrifice,
a geometrical inversion,
an image of a sin
waiting to be forgiven,
a cosmic playing card never dealt,

a nymph on a Roman conveyor belt,
a wheel that could not turn,
a bridge too late to burn,
a neurotic eye on an empty page,
a crippled hand on a pressure gauge
You were never
past or present or future,
you were infinity's veil,
a second thought

A STRATEGY OF MIRRORS

of a vagabond god,
you were the shiftless multitude
concentrated into one,
a Lazarus in the rays
of a miscreant sun,
you were film noir,
you were science fiction,
a city built
on the holy ground
of contradiction

LIKE A MARCEL DUCHAMP PAINTING

DEREK J BROWN

If you think the sky is black now
then just wait until October
said the woman at the bar,
I told her I would never
throw a soul from a moving car,
that speaking to her is like pouring
my heart out to a child,
that I never had a friend
who was not tortured,
that love in my eyes
is like a Marcel Duchamp painting
but the world itself seems drawn
by an inconsistent hand,
that sentience can commence
in an unconventional way,
that the very essence of God
is most likely mechanical,
that even robots express compassion,
that screams of doves equate
to the language of insects,
that thieves of time may nourish
sanctities of space,
that humility can be found
in a Humphrey Bogart film,
that I do not wish for anything
to be explained to me

She told me she understood,
maybe even more

than I ever would
Her thriftless eyes said nothing
as she ordered one more drink,
but from her nature rose the image
of a ballerina fainting,
and love to me still seemed
like a Marcel Duchamp painting

BECAUSE

I am not in love with you because life is brief,
or because you have white teeth or because
of your insurgent acquisitions, or because
there is no because or because
of your fire that does not burn or because
of the meanness of the gods or because
of your sea beast legends or your mermaid
compassions, or your Greek sensibilities,
or your existential embrace, or your inter-
galactic pre-cognitive therapy, or your will-
ingness to remain silent when everything-
else is deep in leviathan consultation,
or because of your lack of desperation,
or because of your praying mantis,
or because of your delivering of no answers,
or because of your sacred infidelities,
or because of your isolated muse upon a
cosmic thread, or because of your cypress tree
on the untainted shore of an intangible
glimpse of what might have been Atlantis

DEREK J BROWN

A STRATEGY OF MIRRORS

COSMIC SALT ON AN EARTHLY WOUND

My primitive brain, tuned to Earth's magnetic field,
intermittently transposed, reset and then reset
God's silence here contains its own unique music,
but impassable voices from impassable forests

replay beguiling gibberish, every earthly wound
cries out for cosmic salt, like nefarious gems
from Daliesque heavens disembodied bouquets,
cataclysmic roses, mechanically cascade

A herd of eyes look forward, to primal signs of winter,
to all that can't be touched, cold as Harold Pinter
Some consult their phones to reconstruct their futures,
some are charmed by ants hauling antiseptic leaves

In hands of mannequins, physical laws are held,
carbon monoxide detectors conduits to aliens
The muses are inflamed, all new ideas are hidden
far inside the graveyards, but I can never look there,

I just don't have the time. No light knows of shadow
yet shadow knows of light, or so some eyes suspect
I gaze at someone's wife; I think of life eating life
and seek a bar with booths, cheap whiskey, no windows

EQUIVALENT OF A BLANK PIECE OF PAPER

A giant dumpster, gold bricks buried in the trash,
sits oblivious to the graveyard's sentiments,
high on the horizon loom the tombstones,
above gilded gates a tenement window
obscures black
and white keys of a grand piano
Neutron star mysteries out in force,

a legion of atoms form bonds with nothing,
meta-physicists wait to hear the songs of swans
but the swans are silent and appear motionless,
as dimensions are drawn to immeasurable pits
The architects, slaves to their own constructions,
dart and stutter
through numberless points of light,

watch all that they must covet recoil into existence
A drunkard approaches, mutters in my ear,
says a truth badly told can never defeat
a lie that comes from red wined lips, I then withdraw
to the most violent serenity, pray for someone
to desecrate my fears, sins as meaningless
as anyone's. I think of you,

a half-assembled jigsaw puzzle, I know you are a symbol
for the dream that I am home, ruptures of beauty,
brittleness of grace, without them
we'd end up sanctified to death. We wait to suffer

DEREK J BROWN

A STRATEGY OF MIRRORS

a moment in which we do not suffer
as phantom musicians consider lost notes,
nurture beliefs there is purpose in futility. All that is visible

projects impression of glass, sacrament made subject
to obviations of wombs, and still there is anarchy of ants,
fruitfulness of flies. Justice wants charity,
charity wants justice, mentalities of reason shelter in absurd
There are secrets too poetic, never-ending theorems
of a nourishing despair, everything remains the equivalent
  of a blank piece of paper

CITY IN MIST, 6:27 AM

From what must be a dream exogenic lights,
strange columns on the fringe of a gaseous border,
revelation's rooms secrete a stench of silence,
locks are in keys, walls become floors

Morning seems biblical, souls sick with gravity,
titans drowned in a post-modern madness,
democracy a baby starved of oxygen, a legion of ears
strain to hear the ticking of a silent clock, this

must be the time to pass the time by corrupting time
Mythologies explode into tiny shards of truth,
nuclear detectives hunt invisible particles, perhaps
the moon will soon dissolve on the bosom of the world,

leave its memory to the sun as constellations curse
And still there are loopholes of this still-life sense,
gold-plated innocence intersecting diamond guilt,
an infinity of numbers the numberless destroy,

a simplicity to sadness complicating joy
All instruments made to play premeditated melodies,
is it Hades? The gestures of God's hand?
Some laws were created broken, do calculating mirrors

calculate themselves? Close to where the light falls
some souls shall be awakened, some shall go to sleep,
it was designed this way. In these cribs of dead desire
flesh still feels warm, there is the impression of a pulse

WINTER RAIN

Tonight, in the city, a winter rain
falls heavily, with an unknown purpose
It takes more than rain to cleanse soul
and more than soul to change a world
pleading to be altered. Everything is
conscience denied its head and tail,
Edward Hopper in his grave,
not turning, not stirring,
tuned to a silence that's heavenly
At times an image will paint itself,

tonight's colour neon,
even the darkest shadow
wields a luminosity
Charcoal sycophants in their rage
can rage forever, I,
beyond my own rage, could not care less
I no longer seek epiphany
or salvation in a woman
with a tarot card countenance. Tonight, I am
a bumbling scientist
looking to measure what can't be measured,

mesmerised by the fact some things are alive,
with what I do not know exactly, I just look at them
and know I am dying slowly, but that's no curse,
there is freedom in seeing your own mortality
The barmaid's face shows a porcelain sentiment,

her pulchritudinous body drips abstract information
I sense her sense a suffering
while everyone else pretends
to celebrate what can't be celebrated
I finish my drink, cast my grief,
far past fireworks until it reaches the moon,

disintegrates across its lifeless surface
In sacred ignorance the primal dance
to the meticulous fear of being alive,
to pathogenic clocks ticking furious,
to peculiar alms for the living dead,
to souls at home on bluest borders
I light a cigarette, walk out into winter rain,
still falling with its cryptic purpose,
still falling as if it's never
going to stop

A STRATEGY OF MIRRORS

RED AND YELLOW

Stillness conveying movement with surgical precision
I am witness to your science, one with its own religion
Every fool's song exacts a sweet and hideous love,
this we've always known, no crude lament need prove
that both the sun and moon are equally grotesque,
we pay no attention; we engage the statuesque,

we mingle among the artists, no secret do they tell,
every work, a self-portrait, a facetious wish for Hell
And we are our own aloneness, each door fascinates,
but every room's prosaic and holds no valid weight
All that is dead today will be dead tomorrow
Red relents to red just as yellow yields to yellow

Neuro-harmonies point the way to a place of self-descent,
the invention of an age where there is nothing to invent
Dragonflies draw flame into strangely vacant space
Handmaids spell the ageing of each immortal face
Conveyor belt processions feed hypnagogic jerks
So tragic, so sadistic, lies the vastness of these works

December brings the music of a nurturing derision,
no one has a choice, all are forced to listen
A prophet with a modern face speaks an ancient mind,
claims the only eye that sees is one that's truly blind
And you and I remain here, in the corner of a dark café,
random lines read aloud by a girl in a green beret,

with the mouth of a baroness, eyes of a wounded dog
we see her pastel scream through a monochromatic fog
Is there something here to salvage? In this sad regime
every dream's a nightmare, no nightmare's just a dream
The ghost of Escher follows as we brave the iron streets
Everything now advances in the moment it retreats

DEREK J BROWN

A STRATEGY OF MIRRORS

CENTRAL STATION

Below ciphers of March
a thousand years have passed,
now that memory is controlled
there is nothing to recall,
no phoenix rises,
no sparrow falls,
yet an unremitting blue
breaches dense millennial walls

Here upon the concourse
of a twilight Central Station,
all commuters share
one phantom of sensation,
one hibernating face
By arrival or departure
their destinations parallel,
they pass each other
with meteoric understanding
of something not fully
set in place, but almost

The trains, temporary symbols
for a powerful inertia,
transmit fatal shadows
of serpents at their rest,

ticket machines administer
make-believe totalities,

in illiterate corners
some cry out for parables,
a swarm of eyes fixate
on the LED departure board,
for that one moment aware
everything is transition
or else nothing is. Below

an art-nouveau clock
forever running late,
sub-heavenly fusions scatter,
syncopated lovers wait
A young girl with amber eyes
plays jazz on a black piano,
a trickster enchanted by her
discards his chants and spells
On platforms nomads clutch
intangible possessions,
the thought of losing them
draws sight of Hades' chains
Cherubs of impermanence
lightly touch their talismans,
until glass resembles stone
and stone resembles glass
It continues, we are here,
others were at one time,
and soon will be again,
tied to new equations,
there is no need for magic

THE UNIVERSE HAS COUNTLESS HOUSES

A STRATEGY OF MIRRORS

Like Edward G Robinson said, 'there's nothing like the
smell of rain', Spencer Tracy rails
against infernos fast and deep,
scarlet women wail
at babes that will not weep,
silk Neanderthals with greasy lapels
track the course of evolution. Hart Crane sleeps

on an ocean bed somewhere, we lie awake
to infernal sonatas, we can only guess
the time, in depths of South Lanarkshire
rhyme and half rhyme
scribbled equally in strange remorse
Through grey yet virginal mists
Glasgow renews its vital myths,

both malignant and benign a consecrated paradox
designed to be forsaken, continues to penetrate
simulated bone and flesh. We pretend we are immune
to parasites of clocks, distant drunken voices,
clowns advancing
(in their razzle-dazzle ignorance)
towards some romantically tragic circus

Visions of history altered, Matt McGinn hung,
drawn and quartered, Cary Grant cast out,
exiled on a mythological island, what it might be like
to not have a sorcerer for a friend

We must get away from here, this version of night in stasis,
the universe has countless houses
and those houses countless rooms

DEREK J BROWN

A STRATEGY OF MIRRORS

TORCH SONG

Nothing more to borrow
The only cure is sorrow
No more wine or bread
No legacy for the dead
No martyr for a crown
No hunger for renown

No more avant-garde
No angel, brute or bard
No temple in the sun
No temperature to run
No more blood to bleed
No embryo, no seed

No lily, rose or dove
No fatal sting of love
No prayer on the stone
No resonance, no tone
No science, no friction
No cosmic valediction

No more little death
No chapel of breath
No casting of lots
No grapes or apricots
No passions to ingest
No script, no manifest

No hymn to buzz the ear
No surface left to smear
No mission to abort
Pas plus vivant ou mort
No loss in translation
No land or sea or nation

No lighting of lamps
No holy foot that stamps
No Orphic chain to bind
No theory of mind
No more rpm
No more us or them

No more him or her
No vision left to blur
No sacred sepulchre
No penance or reward
No extant note or chord
No more piano player

No flag or film or layer
No sense of glass or sand
No god's divining hand
No Artemis, no Apollo
Nothing left to borrow
The only cure is sorrow

A STATE OF NOT KNOWING

Memory holes where sins
magically die with time
rendered inaccessible,
wide-eyed devils
steeped in science fiction
seek the last word,

rows of shop dummies
covered in electrolytes
the omnipotent dilettantes
No secrets I should know,
here on these algorithmic streets
a state of not knowing liberates

The newsfeed, it repeats,
strange animals interrogate nature,
spread legends from a petrified forest
I wait for you among archetypes,
litter of one-way tickets,
irreversible admissions

among synaesthesia and murder
and star-crossed reclamation
we may not recognise each other,
we may pass each other by,
with indecipherable recall,
with godlike resignation

The last light between the buildings
moves over me
and others, who may be waiting only
for the sake of waiting,
tethered to broken clocks,
and mythologies of midnight lovers

DEREK J BROWN

MESSIAH

With a drop of rain, a broken compass,
resplendent rags, a straight-faced grin
I kneel and touch an unknown surface
I think of snakes
without their skin

Where on earth are iron mystics
Where in heavens are loyal kings
The want to breathe gets too holistic,
and deathlessness itself,
it sings

Some say that all is even
I say that all is odd
Empires of the hallowed mind
one by one designed to fall

O angel in need of one more conscience
O nameless faceless unending god
O messiah clothed hermetic blue,
demolish this fictitious wall

History won't keep his distance
Eternity, too much she clings
Death is silent, without resistance
and deathlessness itself,
it sings

I close my eyes to this brutal age
of cleanliness and unfilled art
I wake and waltz a dead-beat sage,
a clock around
my timeless heart

DEREK J BROWN

STRANGER ON PROBATION

Long ago it seems
you were a structural engineer
for the Tower of Babel,
now you're a stranger on probation,
alone with flesh and bone
and occasionally a soul

rejecting room temperature
in the old men's drinking den,
on a diet of cheap whiskey
and dry roasted peanuts,
thinking every woman an assassin
or the source of your redemption,

you gaze not unintelligibly
through a window made of squares
at a disinfected moon
in a cobalt sky of April,
comparing lives not lived,
loves of grocery assistants,

ids of psychiatric nurses,
demons of bus drivers,
amulets of barmaids,
chastity of whores,
euphoria of ravens
You recall sylphs of gravity,

how they oh so quickly
alter their appearance
from a grandiose abyss
As if by abstract hands
lights of all the storefronts
switch on simultaneously

and you know you're late for nothing,
you order one more whiskey
and then another, and then another
You keep a pet mouse
in your overcoat pocket,
occasionally you let it out,

it runs across the bar, no one notices
You tell yourself no truth
is ever quite enough,
until it becomes a mantra,
until you're placed upon the moon,
primed for all beyond

DEREK J BROWN

THE DAY GENE VINCENT CAME TO GLASGOW

On the verge of almost reliving
the day Gene Vincent came to Glasgow
I linger, smoking cigarettes
in the Infirmary's dominant shadow,
following randomly time's deceits,
bait and switch of gods,
pulse of constants in my eye,
magnetic ends and odds

furnishing this vast aloneness,
the mystifying value
of a question that can't be answered
Is this not the way it always is?
In the myth that never was
all happenings that happen
happen simultaneously,
science of music whispers,

moonlight's cold infractions
accumulate then zero in
on some epiphany still to be had
Sirius appears to dance
and with its vanities gesticulates,
every ghost is living
in this revision of revision,
this script of what passes for transience

I fill a small yet incurable space,
same one Gene Vincent filled

back somewhere in the 20th Century
I watch lovers escape
into prisons of their visions
I am not immune; I escape into my own
Here in December's mortal grip
I dream sounds from lucent guitars,

howls of infants born in bitterness,
words of drunkards, unseen sages,
everything subject to impulse
of thermodynamic conundrums
It will soon be Christmas Eve,
seems the lights have burned for ages
and it feels like I was there
the day Gene Vincent came to Glasgow

DEREK J BROWN

A STRATEGY OF MIRRORS

ONE DAY EVERYTHING WILL MELT

The Dali clock
hangs over
the phrenological head,
as if it were a Persian rug,
ubiquitous lumps of coal
examined like diamonds
by solicitous eyes
In this deadlock midnight
layer reflects layer
reflects layer
reflects layer,
everything is possible only
in the moment that it isn't

Lipstick stains
of toothless harlots
left on gin and tonics,
street poets read them
like alien hieroglyphs,
in this heliocentric room
a cluster of mouths
put an end to syllables,
lovers of imprecision
dance to the song's shadow,
everything seems profound
on the edge of 3:AM

One day
everything will melt,

circle Orion's Belt,
sorrow, pity and the rest
will not be required,
the piano player's keys
shall all resemble black,
the shyest snake uncoil
in diabolic confidence,
the darkest matter only
seen to resonate
But as for now
my darling, as for now,
plant your soul upon this tongue

DEREK J BROWN

A STRATEGY OF MIRRORS

GYPSY GIRL WITH MANDOLIN

It's approaching half-past midnight,
we cannot help but gaze,
at a gypsy girl with raven eyes
that neither blame nor praise

She holds her mandolin
like the Madonna holds child,
skeletal hands caressing strings,
arteries of the sacred

An audience of mannequins
inexplicably alive,
tied to their own dimension,
this one they can't survive,

dressed in evening clothes
below a high and sterile moon,
in reverence they listen
to the gypsy's cryptic tune

Locked in divine disorientation,
recipients of a mock salvation,
the rats commence to dance,
the serpents are entranced

You say it's down to chance
I say it's down to fate,
that it's probably too late
to divide or to conflate

There is darkness sick of darkness,
grace that's sick of grace,
sounds we recognise,
destined to misplace

The candles far from dying,
tonight is more than you or I,
real or not it's all illusion
why forsake it asking why?

Perhaps the answer lies
in the gypsy girl's eyes,
or in echoes of her mandolin,
drifting thru nothing, thru everything

DEREK J BROWN

ANTITHESIS OF EVERYTHING

Where simplicity fades, I knew I'd find you,
consuming antithesis of everything,
witness to the ripening of a lucent decay,
to the blueness of each equinox

in which quietude and turmoil meet,
conjoin, where humility is its own conceit
and acts of unforgiving equal absolution,
each contradiction its own ghost

I have dared to understand you
but that has made you coarse and bitter,
and so, I initiate your false regression,
to a cold Shahmaran, an impassive Sphinx

Tender witches leave their cards with men,
men with dead hearts but spirited tongues,
both embodiments of a ravaged nature
I drink to them, they drink to me,

yet I find myself returning, to that unnamed
place of inception. I imagine you there still,
waiting, waiting, waiting, for someone who
resembles me, equipped with those secrets

you desire to know, that you can never know
It is the indelible shape of not knowing
that sustains yet keeps us from sustenance
Let hunger be our teacher of virtue

ABSTRACT CURTAINS

DEREK J BROWN

Freud writhes in his beloved dust
Jung dances to his cryptic drummers
But you, my love, do what you must,
within this fractious chain of summers,

expanding as they die, relentlessly,
sustaining what they can't sustain,
and all that ends, ends endlessly,
grateful for its quantum of pain

We scan intently, birds as ghosts
mimicking schemes of heaven,
synergy of unseen hosts,
steady cadence of abstract curtains

Consider these crowds, technologies
synchronous with internal rhythms,
seductions of their sophistries
dismissing all undying prisms,

centreless centres, coreless cores
framed within unfinished eyes,
all these windows, all these doors,
remain unfixed, and yet somehow amplify

whatever it is we continue to miss,
memories of what we were before
this inhuman shift in consciousness,
this science lovers in their glaze ignore

A STRATEGY OF MIRRORS

absorbing itself in the blood of us,
renewing needlessly its nebulous vows,
and the primal heart's dark abacus,
carefully miscounting whatever it allows

ALEXANDER HUTCHISON

Alexander Hutchison
said 'everything is vanishing'

Chekhov and his chocolates
Whitman and his beard
Onyx and obsidian
What cannot be cohered
The heart below the table
The mind above the rim
The viciously angelic
The nature of each limb

Humility of magic
Religion of bone
Science of flesh
Evils to condone
Atoms in their meekness
Ravens and crows
Hawks and sparrows
Gods in their repose

Even death is vanishing
Vanishing into death
Across paths of deviation
And apogees of spheres
Across a nothingness that wages
Across a wilderness of tears
Across an age of Christmas nights

DEREK J BROWN

And prognosis
And dissection
And neutralities of bliss
Alexander Hutchison said
'everything is vanishing'

And so, it is

THE GLASS HARMONICA

Behind a blackout curtain
a glass harmonica hides,
preordained to hear
its convoluted strains
I knew you would appear,

you had no choice
An entire life caesura,
what must be the soul
in a blown glass vessel,
it generates its algorithms
like there was
no eternity

Take this body,
bruise it until it heals
Take your myths,
unite them in flesh
There is no telling
what I misconceive
You call seductively

to a universe
whose ears are full of wax
Quintessential orphan
you raise your holy hands
to the follies of the world
Instruct your threadbare czars
to play their dead guitars
I will pretend to listen

A STRATEGY OF MIRRORS

RANDOM NUMBER GENERATOR

Things are so predictable you call yourself a psychic,
have a mass of broken minds fall at your unwashed feet,
a child's simple puzzle declared a doorway to the soul
In another age you served, in the temple of Hecate,

where light and darkness were lovers, where evolution
was a measureless circle, but happiness can pierce your side
like a cruel, relentless sword, lifeboats carriers
of absolute demise, sometimes inhumanity

possesses its own form of elegance, sometimes memory is
an entity unto itself, ask the ghost of Whitman
or Anthony Bourdain, tragic is not inedible
Sometimes you're better off

in the snow, in the rain, drunk on champagne. At whims
of a random number generator, you whisper in my ear,
the sound of your voice more meaningful
than any word it utters, some worlds seem hidden

when in fact they lie spread-eagled, naked in the open
Not every dot supposed to be connected, you clasp your
  hands
before me while behind you the trickster coughs
and I realise it is possible to suffer without suffering

Like a procession of Christs with no memory of the Cross
dreams of never having dreamed dissolve
and you and I sink deeper in absurd, ever constant

states of internal transit, primordial reflexes
Always the dead within us and we within the dead,
but sometimes liberty can never be part of a song,
there is no rule that says it must. Below sanctities of dust
I look towards you and know there are no more words
  between us

A STRATEGY OF MIRRORS

DYSLEXIC BIRDS IN OLYMPIC DULLNESS

Dyslexic birds in Olympic dullness,
the appearance of the death's head moths
having accomplished nothing, I scan hallowed
cancerous streets, dying metaphors,
skeletal synonyms, I wait for you
knowing if you come I will not know you
I will blame it on the climate
and paralytic promise
of snow then rain, snow then rain,
recalling rapture, alchemy of your limbs,
delectations of your runic red lips
recalling your kiss on my untaught brow,
a demigod's whisper to a drowning superego
Mystical doors pretend to open,
sudden windows
materialize out of pity. I await still,
like a totalitarian statue in a devastated place,
a you that was
not you

NABOKOVIAN

The blood moon's waves religiously dissolve,
after-paths of clouds on twilight glass,
but these neon interventions do not shrink,
dollhouses in the distance loom so vast

In primal hours prolonged, in odd fragilities,
alpha floats detached from its omega,
befouled statues, in Russian evening,
spring to life, go swimming in Ammonia

And no voice speaks of heaven or of earth,
that is justice in a void where all's unjust,
angels pray profusely to be wingless,
physicists anoint themselves with dust

All rules are now illusion, illusion is the rule,
everything transmits sublimely static,
puppeteers guide synesthetic ghosts,
conterminous with eyes immune to magic

We pass beyond lonely sun-downed martyrs
devouring sacred figs and luminous pears,
unveiling all those things they love to covet,
such clowns of deprivation, with all their cares,

who or what would profit from their pain?
Legions of gods, none of them intelligible,
synchronized like clocks in sterile rooms,
religion of empty spaces born indelible

A STRATEGY OF MIRRORS

ANATHEMA

I sit here by the window
in the Libertine café,
watch crows that perch
on corrugated fences,
artificial afterlives
Fathomless lovers hook
themselves to a sense of vertigo,
hands of summer

paint serpent hearts that hide
reasons why they beat
Martyrs stand amazed
by their love for Anathema,
she reclines oblivious
to upside-down desires
I sneer at my redemption,
resist hours that propel me

to precisions of past
Various instruments cornered
bask in silence finely tuned,
one that hangs opposed
relentlessly to itself,
except to chains of voices
in demented sequence
speaking as if they're speaking

hyperphysical language
Strange eroticisms escalate

sensual putrefaction,
until the entire scene resembles
a kind of Cubist painting
Hosts of cancelled equations
in unremitting hesitations,
those addicted to thirst
sip from empty cups,

the deathless here may choose
the moment of their death
All crows have vanished,
linear now in the grip
of alien forms of gravity
A sadness here sustains
its very own antithesis

DEREK J BROWN

NONCHALANT FIXATION ON A
NAKED BALLERINA

My will for now is spent,
waits to be refilled,
by a virago predisposed
to a neon kind of instinct
Black eyed sweethearts gather
at the Laughing Cat café,
rewrite laws of physics,
contest hearts of atoms
I expect to hear fake news
of some new flying machine,

everything rests
on an imagination
crazier than reality
I create the mind of God
the way a painter paints
his nonchalant fixation
on a naked ballerina
City streets elapse
into beautiful inertia,
hands of widows grasp
sacrilegious galaxies,

course of rain resents
density of stone
Monosyllabic minstrels,
subterranean romantics

centre on tunes
of a midnight concertina,
some of them in love
with anaesthesiologists,
others righteously engaged

in integrity of their own
self-destruction
It was designed in me to pass
these advocates of glass,
simulated sense of concrete,
counterfeit spaces,
dissections of natures
of things that have no nature
Xanthippe, come forth,
inflame your final ecstasy

DEREK J BROWN

THE MYTHOLOGY OF PROGRESS

Dancers improvise
to the strangest music,
in and among champagne glasses,
intangible,
immeasurable,
loves of unknown origins
permeate, transcend
everything that is
process or terminal,

as you linger before me
in space of words
neither written nor spoken,
neither read nor heard
The dancers continue
dancing to another age,
that you and I
had perhaps long ago lived through,

perhaps didn't,
no passion dies
except within its deadness
And now that all is perpendicular
the dancers brave the circles,
false perimeters,
vertigo heavens,
mythology of progress

Beyond masks of chlorophyll
and hierarchal lilies
I watch you still,
thru foreplays of lies,
intrigue of sighs,
always dying
monumental
temporal,
convex walls
of a concave universe

DEREK J BROWN

GOSPEL OF THE NOTES AND KEYS

Plunged deep in disbelieving blue,
nights are full, days are empty,
white roses perish in red euphoria,
and you no more are worth wanting,

here in metropolitan darkness
where those who sleep will never wake
because they do not know they sleep,
they do not hear the purest music,

gospel of notes and keys,
sound religiosities
City station sycophants
in need of no real destination

in a place brimming with small epiphanies
arriving at their own distinctive shadows,
knotted faces of reasonless lovers
fall in and out of righteous focus

Soon a strange announcement
of things on time that should not be,
reasons without a grain of mercy,
mercies without a grain of reason

And still I refuse to desire you,
for in your mind my desire contracts
and expands in cold synchronicity
It is a game and not a game,

with rules, without rules,
your eyes negate their psychic objects,
your limbs convey their physical lies
I have examined all your subjects,

cephalopods, strange octopi,
your jewels, their bastard colours,
your drunken moths in a dead moon's light
Your thoughts and memories my own,

traversing together stars and rain
and phoenix flames, we have been brave
as leopards, nervous as white deer,
our guts twisted by gossamer hands

Touching love's vermillion
in acrylic afternoon, we have passed
Spring's end and stopped just beyond. All is well,
all is good, this is a letter that will never be sent

BUDDHA UNBECOMING

3AM this morning
Buddha appeared,
I climbed out of bed,
offered him a slice of bread,
he took it, asked me
do you have any butter?
I said sorry, I had run out
Behind a broken window
a sparrow's wings
commenced to flutter,
Buddha ate the bread,
said it was rather tasty,

wiggled his head,
blinked his eyes twelve times,
looked somewhat thin,
spoke nothing of sin,
said his belly ached,
that he could think of nothing
but food
He spoke of strawberry tarts
and lemon cheesecake
and chocolate chip ice cream,
spoke of pancakes

doused in golden syrup,
of Russian caviar
and Rockefeller oysters,
of Camembert and truffles,

sirloin steak and French fries,
he spoke of all sorts
of culinary delights
I told him all I had
was that single slice of bread,
he nodded his head,
said he understood,
that it was all for the good,
that everything depends
on a dose of cosmic laughter
and a morsel of starvation,
that we are all in our own ways

Buddhas unbecoming,
to sentiments of the stars,
planets made to shatter
mirrors of themselves
It was then that I asked him
who or what was God,
he replied that no one knew,
that all shall be redeemed
by its own grip on futility

He said he had to leave now,
he had an appointment in Las Vegas,
where he likes to dress in drag,
and puff on big cigars

DEREK J BROWN

A STRATEGY OF MIRRORS

IN MEMORY OF THE PRESENT

One thousand years of thinking
an interlude of thought,
we are fractions
of a looking-glass
scattered under sun

In memory of the present,
blue sonatas sweep
designated boundaries,
like black, unmarked helicopters
on occult manoeuvres
The clocks have gone insane,

strategically arranged
in a banishment of time,
no hours or minutes,
not even seconds
pass before the sorry ranks
of the men and the women
mimicking snakes and lizards

In toy-town torture chambers
post-industrialists play
demonic musical chairs,
the mirror of each movement
proudly shows its cracks,
with a shrunken hippocampus
and a craving for inanition

consumers quickly move
from shimmering floor

to shimmering floor,
sanitation experts
encroach like Hell's octopus,
tentacles reaching
the invisible corners
On metaphysical streets
self-liquidising Homers
exhale their final breaths,
the vagabonds sing
of dark secrets in
the hands of glass,
of the immorality of silence

DEREK J BROWN

A STRATEGY OF MIRRORS

IMAGE OF YOU DESCENDING

This is not a portrait,
I barely recall your face,
or where I was exactly
when you claimed human nature
was a poem stripped of metaphor

In green chrysanthemum night
you slowly descend stairs,
from where all is but inverted,
planetary puppet-shows,
reconstructed stars

Your mind a sacred text
I read a million times
but could not understand
I travelled on a thousand myths,
searched for sophic hydroliths

I was excited for a taste of you
knowing I would thirst again
Across trails of cosmic mimicry
glide fragments of your life,
like microscopic crystals
flashing intermittently

As if my every thought
were a knife that could not cut
not even your weakest element

I had no choice but to retreat,
to an image of you descending
in green chrysanthemum night

DEREK J BROWN

COURSES ECHOES TAKE

I do not know
what kind of shadow fell,
my relationship to light
a complicated one
You were quite content
to belong to nothing,
an angle of perspective
from an anamorphic hill,
you were what happened
when the world became too still
And laced between the pages
of a strange and boundless book
memory knows of nothing
but the imprint of itself

Eyes were never windows,
hands could not atone,
no guidance of flesh
when all consists of stone,
no vision for feeding,
no virtue to extol,
no virtuoso reading
of a hieroglyphic soul,
there is only observation
and courses echoes take,

ghosts of words and names
on tips of tide-less tongues,

an absence of reply,
a dream that wields no wake

DEREK J BROWN

A STRATEGY OF MIRRORS

THE BARBARITY OF GLASS

No destiny our destiny,
we have our own remorse,
leave alone the sleepless
to build a tower
they'll never climb,
illegalise the clocks
until there is no time

We will study flowers
as if they'd grown on Mars,
drown ourselves in honey,
watch the pantomime
from front row
with a straight face

The barbarity of glass
is humility of sand,
all is subservient,
to circle within circle,
wheel within wheel,
irrefutable
rhythms of biology

And you my darling
are a blackbird,
I gaze at you a thousand ways,
now look me in the eye,
the only myth that counts
is the myth there is no myth

Whistle to me blackbird,
whistle until night comes
in all its indecipherable worship
It is almost time to fly

DEREK J BROWN

THE SEAGULLS OF SAUCHIEHALL STREET

A woman clings to my oneness
She holds my silence
She holds it like the pose of a 1930s starlet
She holds it like a drunkard holds his wine,
allowing nothing to constrain
(except that which must)
remembering to bypass
each edifice of memory,
every ghetto of transcendence,
to let each force of nature
honk, scream, whisper

I saw her in Merchant City
talking to herself,
wearing a mask or two,
advocating mystery
that says there is no mystery,
her eyes absorbing things all other eyes reject,
present only in an absence
that controls these mannequins,
shadow-puppets caught by an alternating sun

The seagulls of Sauchiehall Street
know they're flying in a day that dreams,
I forgive their trespasses,
they too are oppressed
by the thought of not being so
Alexander Greek Thomson laughs hysterically,

nowhere to the point of tears,
just to the point of knowing
he's not present on any table,
he's nowhere to be seen
Is he observing Mona Lisa pluck her eyebrows?
Is he pressing tulips in a book by Dostoevsky?
Is he drowning in a sea of his own construction?

Spectres in abandoned office spaces
dictate a constant brevity
Synchronicity moves
in and out of ears
and eyes
and hands
A thousand shadows tumble
back into their hovels,
waiters take away
half-empty glasses,
on white napkins
ragged men pen mood poems,
hundreds of miles from here
ancient burial stones
shift like hands of clocks,
history passes and passes,
movement of history present here always,

brushing lightly against spines
of almost unseen places,
brushing against drama queens
in resplendent dresses,

A STRATEGY OF MIRRORS

moving to strings
of cerulean guitars,
moving to slight tremors,
passions underground,
moving to voices persecuted by their words

And still this woman clings to my oneness,
this woman whose name I do not know,
nor do I care to, her anonymity alone hypnotic
I fall back into a consciousness I sense is somehow just

THE HEAD OF A PIN

You look for a hand to swing a pendulum,
a voice to hypnotise and tell you
you will never again be hypnotized,
that you are a creature that offers reason
But the flower and the tree are not for you,
the rock and the glass, they are not for you,
the unimpeachable day
is not for you

In an incandescent kingdom darkness is essential,
no word is ever full, no page is ever blank,
scent of bitter lemon an abstract pleasure,
there is no sorrow that will not be imagined,
the way that we arrive is not the way that we depart,
the pallbearer does not know he is emphasizing Christ

No more need for oracles
or wishing wells,
everything now depends
upon the edge of silence,
on the head of a pin and so much more

A STRATEGY OF MIRRORS

BELOW A MOON OF SOFT SUSPENSE

I kiss in my delirium
a mathematic mouth,
one whose lips are tainted,
whose cryptic sorrow crosses
each convoluted curve,
each sliver of dark matter-
every seed of mindless joy,
beyond cherry blossoms,
dishonest fragrance,
beyond lethal eyes of doves
and rotting strings of jewels,

its chilling and perfect body,
whose flesh cannot atone,
prays love won't be disturbed
by its own depraved illusion
or shapeless supple idols
sick and tired of worship,
or by lighting of incense
when dark and light concur,
this cold and sublime body
ignores living and dead,
requires no admission,
has no choice but to continue,
sustain itself and seek
language sans design,
to place and underline
silent strange new genesis

BEYOND THE SENSE OF ASHES

All are words, quickly they decay,
into silences, spaces that persist,
amnesias singing of day
A world without death,
a measure of dissent
a measure of applause,
fury signifies; nothing is everything,
an ascendancy of eyes
pursuing beauty, so soon struck down,
no moment of resistance
in hours where mystery recoiled,
among eternity's dead phrases,
in hours of harshest definition,
still beyond a sense of ashes
whispers now a world of language,
neither time nor sand,
neither space nor glass,
comes soon another world
not born yet still must pass,
all that was – your sovereignty of sight,
all that can remain without remaining,
in meaninglessness of names,
once, we were nameless,
now, forever aging

DEREK J BROWN

IMPENETRABLE WHISPERS OF A
THIN-SKINNED NUDE

I say nothing
I have nothing to say,
the stillness of my words
institute your whiteness,
upon raven leaves,
starless sheets
of alien principality

O how you let them draw you,
dressed to kill neanderthals
pretending they'll survive
ferocities of clocks
O how you let them paint you

Vixens are transfixed
by their own impaired reflection,
leavings of a wretch
dictate to what surrounds them,
sealed in your elegant agony
to you they are not there

I study strange discrepancies
between your body and your soul
I turn from your flesh,
in a golden age of poverty
your Gordian whispers
delineate me and remain

Nothing now is liberated
but shadows born of liberties,
existence of things inside
things that don't exist,
I dream a new foundation
no more a dream than you

A STRATEGY OF MIRRORS

PHYSICALITY OF WATER

Physicality of water
outweighs all depth of fire,
this is no enigma,
not like the world we know exists
but were not designed to find,
where everything shifts
within its own disfigured confines
I comprehend you without knowing,
crystal decreases crystal
until the only myth there is
is the one that is grotesque,
for which lovers slay archetypes
or else convert them into stone,
glorify all that spawns
from the lie that all's subjective
There is the darkness of a mirror
and the mirror of a darkness,
does it matter
which one the eye peers into?
This question is your answer
and your answer is this question
and that cannot be changed

ORDER OF THE LOCUSTS

Here at this mockery
of predestination
you are somewhat near me,
fastened
to an effigy of yourself,
uncalculated,
like the ambience
of a universe invisible
You have studied consciously
the order of locusts,
consulted thermionic ghosts,
retinas,
colonies of eyes contracted
in mass-produced surprise
I wish my heart
was on Machu Picchu
or in throes
of crisscrossing discreetly
enigmas of the Nazca Lines
When your own
mystery is reduced
to a hydrostatic skeleton
how then shall I respond?

DEREK J BROWN

THE ALETHEIA WITHIN YOU

Coarse compassions at your fingertips,
across pedantry of spectrum,
rebellions of blue,
the mimicry of your painter's palette
ambuscading deviations,
precision of inexactness
scrambling to define you,
like a hunter's moon determined
to supersede itself

Luminous but sinister,
fatal but remote,
the dereliction of a conscience,
a temperature rising
in the instance that it falls,
a pyrexia that finds its climax
in a sphinx-like state of calmness,
the Aletheia within you

SENILE WOMAN IN THE CORNER

In these blue surroundings that melt
like snows that vanished with March,
the senile woman in the corner
sings a sweet and incomprehensible song,
not completely unwelcome visitors
consult phantoms of each other,
ones with nothing left to haunt
but voids left by absence,
in a space where nothing is recorded
but the mad and shapeless voice
of a god who has forgotten our memory,
it recalls only its incontrovertible shadow
masked by crude festivities designed
to replicate the mystery
that these ignorant eyes call light

DEREK J BROWN

A STRATEGY OF MIRRORS

THE VERY FIRST DAYS OF FEBRUARY

The chequerboard is elevated,
there is a heavenly displacement
where I sit inside this bar,
the patrons talk of nothing
but masquerades of circumstance,
essentially oblivious
they know not to be thankful
A crucial aimlessness lingers,
like alcohol on the breaths
of the cryptically broken-hearted,
they nurture each other's grief
like a messiah his tender garden

The dog beside me whines,
perhaps it knows
what I do not know
and do not wish to know,
but not everything is a graveyard
or cemetery insight
I sit here and recall the snow
The very first day of February
did not completely turn to night

CITY CHAMBERS MASQUERADE

DEREK J BROWN

Dismissing sand and glass, I await ancient certainties,
I hear the gossip of gods, their taunting symmetries,
inhuman tempos, inbred rhythms. The seats of the theatre
occupied by vacancies manufactured to implode
The wonder that is gravity is threatening to collapse

A member of the council recites a poem by Robert Burns
In the stomach of the city immense conundrums churn
In doorways beggars faces bleed an odd contentment
There are eyes inside of clouds; there are things no eyes
  cement

This the western mystery, a memory commenced at night
pretends to dissipate in light
that streams from centreless interiors, creeping
thru hints of love and madness and perjuries of diamond
  hearts
An emancipation stops and starts

and stops to bitter, deep agendas, Japanese tourists
  photograph
the Scott monument, Thomas Campbell's statue, the
  Cenotaph
A sign of some hurricane eclipse of the moon collides with
  stone walls
A silence crooked as death, desecrates its own breath, rises
  and falls

A STRATEGY OF MIRRORS

and rises, a procession of cars without passengers or drivers
moves with its own intent, as if trying to stop these days
from devolving into hours then into seconds
where every proton and neutron are tabulated
The laws of human nature resemble keys on a toy piano,

things anomalous hide within sediments of justice,
a night without dreams comes constantly descending
from parapets undying, unparalleled cryptic domes
The stench of psychic flowers
circulates through cracks and grates, open windows
through which is seen no face but the countenance

no conscious hand could frame. Chronometers of the lonely,
birds on heads of statues, intellects in tombs,
trumpets of them and us, harmoniums of him and her,
involuntarily let slip an illusory exterior
Countless times I've been here yet it feels like the first time
Half a foreigner, half a citizen, is there stairs that I must
    climb?
Leading to some colonnade adorned with demons, bards and
    angels

It is the mind that is electric; it is the body sung that's limp
I know it through these streets, deathless thoroughfares
where god-forsaken imps partake of questionnaires
From unrelinquished rain, upon the language of stones
fall unmitigated shadows, obstreperous unknowns
Amid litanies of survival, amid reversible religions,
can patriotism save my soul? Is it time to feed the pigeons?

ANOTHER ATTEMPT AT A LOVE POEM

With your Roman neck
and Spanish head,
with your Greek mouth
and German eyes
you beguile me, you torment me,
into not submitting,
I submit anyway,
not becoming one,
instead becoming two,

for bone is bone
and flesh is flesh
I am forced now to dream
of what I do not know
but am supposed to know,
some future life
that lasted for one second,
of a world where glass
is not sacrilege to sand,
of a vision in the eye
of a blackbird,
of Renaissance art,
of evil hands and angel hair,
the energies of all
sworn in as death,
of what must be forgiven,
of a Hell that must be Heaven

DEREK J BROWN

A STRATEGY OF MIRRORS

PARTICLES AND WAVES

Not Joan of Arc, or Cleopatra,
or Persephone, something irreligious,
chronically suspended from
the myth of a fifth element,

something beautiful, viciously immutable
In celestial museums whose walls
should be a little less full, energy dies

and doesn't, there are the usual
particles and waves, mute taste, blind touch,
chapped lips pressing on nothing, porcelain
contemplation, dignity of dead dolls

There are mountains, there are rocks
There is Laurel, there is Hardy. There is
Chico, Harpo, Groucho, Gummo, Zeppo

and Karl Marx, a constant, carefully
regulated speed, a sea whose floor is cruel,
an eternal kiss upon a mythical brow

SLEEPING MAN ON A RED COUCH

Sleeping man sees the physics, one state of energy to yet
  another,
traverses particles as they taunt and shift, no encore
  renders unique
the mannequins' witching hour assault, although
awareness is treadmill, and the end
of the dark hall quickens away and away. There are voices
  that say

death is no big deal, but the sleeping man cracks
like a grandmother's China, anticipates a secret
uncompressed chamber, where a weeping clown
plays piano with crustacean hands
and a rose-cheeked lady feeds her pet dragon,

where Lucifer's lawyers pull out their flashlights,
go in search of tomorrow, O the sheets of sorrow
are stained with an illiteracy so bizarre it could pacify a tiger
Sleeping man on a red couch
suspects that he is dreaming, that here is nothing

at all that is too familiar, except maybe the gravity
of the carousels and Ferris Wheels, all that the thief never
  steals
He's a babe in the woods
of the Frankfurt School of Science, a grand old duke of dark
  he lurks
Intentionally deaf to thunderclaps of unimpaired compliance,

he descends, having swallowed the moon,
from a primal mountain, speaks an unrecognized language
Like a trickster he presses
against religion of tides, chains himself
to himself, thru parlour games

of grooms and brides, as the Great Whore of Babylon,
on the verge of her geology, regurgitates, as if by apology
O sleeping man, would you
ride a glass elevator to a blacktop sky
Would you kiss the girls just to make them cry?
O sleeping man, sleep,

until the mouse runs up the clock, sleeping man, sleep, sleep!

LADY WITH THE BROKEN LAPTOP

The dervish in the white robe dances, on the concourse
of Indoctrination Central, looks up and down only,
saves compassion for broken minutes
accumulating at his unclean feet
He has been here many times before,
he will be here again, until every trickster

asphyxiates on its own strange humility
Crows vacate dreams,
pigeons grow disgruntled, just like always,
the statues in George Square
seem to show affinity,
traffic vanishes into itself,
parasites pay tributes

to undyingness of storefront dummies
Like a domesticated hyena she shrieks,
the lady with the broken laptop
in the Terminal Café, feeds
on newsfeeds that provide her ultra-meaning,
perches above a soiled floor,
dreams a one eyed, one-armed sister

Drenched in yellow she moves
between the whiteness of the walls,
fondles commemorative bracelets
on her spindling blue-veined wrists, she calls
to the lonesome barista, with her delicate

DEREK J BROWN

A STRATEGY OF MIRRORS

smothering eyes,
he magically fails to answer,

prepares instead a misfit's Americano,
temporarily kills the memory of last night's draconian
  pageant
It is Sunday, early afternoon,
precognition cascades down dry and pale parameters,
the masters of surveillance have pennies for eyeballs
It can't always be this way, evolution has ulterior motives,
crows and pigeons sense this, even sparrows possess an
  insight

OF MEMORY

The way you looked at the blackbird
has stayed with me,
where contentment stings,
where sorrow cures,
where lightning strikes
painlessly,
invisibly

Tranquilised by tranquillity,
on the cusp of what seems like the moon
held by a demon hand,
the only memory I have of you
is when you stripped yourself of memory

and of memory
and of memory…

WINDOWS

A STRATEGY OF MIRRORS

The sleepless sleeper stands, his back to a new oblivion,
not by reason or perfection must he wait the birth of proof

Stations of time unlit, owe to blinding colours
a particle of their shelters, a shadow of themselves

Each philosopher gnaws on bones of the oblivious
One absinthial liberation, one covenant of nature

Another weeping woman casts her offspring to the moon
Another phantasy reacts to the song and dance of death

Civic beams transcend temper of their inexactness
Penniless merchants cling to bourgeoisie insensates

The illiterates write books, the blind paint blues and reds
Architects wear masks, surgeons sketch disease

Unanimous, alive and dead, Byronic cardboard cut-outs
for one second intersperse, eternally doubt eternity

God himself pedestrian sees all windows in one window
The reason for our penance must reproduce itself

SOUND OF A SUBWAY TRAIN HEADING EAST

DEREK J BROWN

The spectre of our liberty,
for now, must not be seen,
we stand inside a space
where we will never cease,
sound of a subway train
heading forever east,

an insect annotates
the human dance of desire,
midnight's room reshaped
hosts a series of mirrors,
set up to distort,
mutate our dream of time

There is a looming question
of what exactly happens
when truth is forced to hide
below a terminal scent of love,
the city a laboratory
whose experiments are moot,

its synergetic diamonds
no longer shine so brightly,
promise kept by sunlight
soon is broken by the moon
A dry sleep in our eyes,
ghost saliva in our mouths,

A STRATEGY OF MIRRORS

we are serfs, subservient
to all that can't be measured
We make our graveyard calls,
our requests unto the ether,
but the dead do not respond,
for it would be sacrilege

The intangible becomes tangible,
a candle that never burns,
until all is out of sequence
and through necessity returns,
to the sound of a subway train
heading forever east

EVERYTHING IS PARADOX

DEREK J BROWN

Tonight, the lamps are blazing, shadows lose themselves,
all that was called human has now been rearranged,
definitions have been altered, but you and I remain,

a necessary nothingness isolating us together
occasionally corrects itself, re-examines, modifies,
reconciles our time and space, but come my love

and follow me, compassion won't convert you,
no eye would dare invert you; no hand could realign you,
grief will not confine you; I will cover you,

feed you with pale moonlight, exhilarated sorrows,
sobs of callous ecstasies. In this curious dimension
presence seen as absence, absence seen as presence,

everything is paradox. Dismiss all past sincerities,
assign them to the death song of an obsolescent season
This is the way it is now; I am forced to empathise,

I too am suffering this unwillingness to suffer,
this worship of the self, ownership of flesh,
consecrated shamelessness, the sad elimination

of what was tagged as madness. Now that innocence is guilt
and guilt is innocence I promise to preserve you
I will lead you to a place where they will never find you

SATURNALIA OF CHAOS

It's a typical day,
it's a twilight day,
lovers of plutonium
begin their new religion,
trees resent their leaves,
waterfalls flow upward,
bridges are short,
roads and avenues horizontal

Take me for a walk,
I'm a cultural dog
seeking Id exploding closure,
or affection from a whore
in a sickly white kimono
I'm a child of astronomy,
a victim of graffiti

I'm ready to join the circus,
saturnalia of chaos,
its destitute acrobats,
charcoal clowns,
zoological freaks
Beyond all sense of construct,

O goddess of geometry,
I will walk on your hot coals,
defenestrate myself,

gladly embrace fundaments
of systematic extinction

After all, it's only a movie!

PHYSIOLOGY IS STRANGE

I lie here dreaming
your invertebrate love,
how it shapes me, its spineless compassion,
compassion nonetheless. I cannot wake,
physiology is strange and verging on mystery

The machines are prescient, cognizant threats,
flesh feels infinite, bone seems boundless,
marionettes drenched in cosmic perfume,
the rest indelible inconsistency

Starving mouths whisper, they say to devour
is to strengthen the truth of a myth ever dying
I devour you, although my stomach is weak
I look at you, an impoverished reflection

in a place of blind opulence. Reiterations
of a savage evolution surround me and I
wait for you where waiting
will not, must not, discriminate in its danger

LOVE IS JUST A SUNDOG...

I remember I felt something, something orbiting
alien sentiment, something unutterable,

I was reconstructing something as irreparable as time
I was reading a book about empty space,

how there was no such thing, you made me want to
wear the philistine's hat, you made me want to

seek refuge in cave dweller doctrines,
but thank god for synchronicity, I saw a door

in my mind's eye, to strains of *Love Her Madly*,
and I knew there was no mind

(just burlesque of serendipity)
and I knew there was no eye

(just mockery of chance)
I am at the mercy of your predetermined dance,

not below the moonlight or crudeness of the sun
but a dance sympathetic to needs of mannequins

I am not one to hang on whims of completeness
I'd rather hear counting of unaccountable numbers,

not hear you say what I am positive you just said,
that love is just a sundog, a temperature inversion

GLISSANDO

No music here, no necromantic strings,
no grey, no ghost of fog or steam,
a lostness only, indolent immeasurability,
insignias of a last rite's dream

All industry enchained, the city's heart
not bright or dark, just blind, shackled
to its own incommunicable colour. No towers of ash,
no monuments of dust, just terminal voices

wailing over coffins
of their candled and saccharine time
But tomorrow is never lost, those that say it is
are addicted to glass cathedrals, funerals in their minds,

and in their eyes grind the engines of their lies
Irradiated starlets vomit love for Karl Marx,
fly by night messiahs require blood transfusions,
ethanol lotharios crave the Bronte sisters,

sterile Madonnas trim their delicious eyebrows,
nightjars are filled with stems of sunflowers,
madmen sleep in rooms with no discernible walls
I know that you are present, beyond silent bodies

of eurybathic beasts, beyond the shape of sickness
and autonomy of ghosts, clear of morbid lights
and all destructive force. Far above what I emit
you unleash your remnant storm, glissando, cruciform

BLUE INFINITY ON MAIN STREET

DEREK J BROWN

Is this where we seek forgiveness? Or refill once more the
  glass?
Below iron virtues and morality of stone, this injured
  imitation,
mimicry of space, parody of time, this ever-changing street

This is where you worship, venerate the god of vanity
But your works cannot deny their critical futility
Your eyes will not disturb the essence of humanity

Above the painted shadow and fugitive reflection,
look closer, you'll see God, reinvent his reinvention,
a bloodied mouth determined to regenerate its speech,

a damaged hand still striving to reach and grasp its legacy
I have been staring far too long into the Town Hall windows,
predisposed to linger beneath its insolent and timeless clock

I dream of lies that secretly nurse wounded truth,
apparitional distance between oblivion and oblivion
I observe the dance of chameleons, their prehensile tails,

long extensible tongues, parietal eyes
I watch as they disseminate their mystery convictions. It is
  here,
afterbirth of a conscience that delivers and preserves,

to fleeting realisations that we are of and not of this world,
this imperfect sphere where everything retreats as it advances,

closes as it opens, destroys as it creates. Its hosts self-
  deceiving,

their adversaries subservient. Is this where we seek
  acceptance?
Or empty the dregs of the cup? Somewhere a voice
recites *The Sermon on the Mount*, or *A Man's A Man for A'*
  That,

or some prayer that's been rewritten a thousand and one
  times

And still the town hall clock mocks and reassigns us,
nefariously incorrupt, truthfully dishonest

SYLLABLES

All is circular,
like the conscience of a man
disturbed by glass streams,
the most luscious destitution

You are alone, I am with you,
we drink from the cup
of such strange contradiction,
syllables of God's subliminal tongue

You split me like an atom,
October accelerates
it's alkaline dreams
I speak of the dead,

the heresy of monoliths,
their cruel syncopations
I am ready to bathe
in your voluptuous futility

DEREK J BROWN

EVERYTHING IS SAD THIS MORNING

Be as simple as a circle
or primitive as a pyramid,
you're at the anteroom of my mind,
you look as if you've
rammed your elbow through a window

Everything is sad this morning,
the wooden birds,
the concrete horses
The age of temptation is over
The centre of beauty ugly

Bind your sign to my forehead,
humiliate the absolute,
punish me with pleasure,
reward me with sorrow

Pretend you're from the Pleiades
or maybe Easter Island
Slip from the cover of darkness
and harness electricity
Consummate meaninglessness
of someone else's meaning

I'm defiant as a mouse,
you wait for a solar eclipse,
lick your sacrificial lips
O when shall you dissect me?
Before or after I fall asleep?

ANTIPATHY OF LAMPS

I've slept through nights of fine white porcelain,
fed the sparrow, killed the mockingbird,
seen synchronicity consume synchronicity,
heard strange arpeggios infect a velvet word

I've witnessed circulations of an animal moon,
cognitive dissonance of a fathoming sun
I've been drawn to eclipses, carnivorous eyes,
irregularities the conscious shun

provocations of serpents, incorruptible sorrows
ominous serenities and spineless threats,
curators of darkness, the antipathy of lamps,
headless bodies, stumbling marionettes

Thru flowers and veils and loves mispronounced
I've trod miscreant hours, supplicated the dead,
absorbed bitter music, absinthian voices,
that say everything is nothing continuously fed

I was once designed and so I must design,
grown blind to outside magic, incandescent altars,
beyond the face that is the mask
and the mask that is the face, a strategy of mirrors

DEREK J BROWN

THE FLESH OF MEMORY

A paradigm falls
I simultaneously
remember and forget,
bypass for a moment
what might be/
might not be
destiny

The radio emits synchronicity
Thank You for The Music
plays what feels forever
I hold your lifeless
incandescent hand,
tender waves of energy
methodically rise and fall
until there is no difference
between what was life
and what was not
I know no more,

what is cruel / what is kind,
here in the mind
a constant voice mutters
about what is one
and what is one
and what is one,

water in the blood,
blood in the water,

order that is chaos,
chaos that is order
I leave this frozen room

Below the moon's articulations
a renegade silence suppresses
night's microcosms,
penetrates stone philistines,
archangels of granite
The bridge between desired
and undesired,
between memory of flesh
and flesh of memory,
extends itself as always
I commit your Delphic mouth,
your hematite crystal eyes

Your partially cryptic body
cries out for nothing
and no one

TINKLING CYMBALS

Heretics from the terminus
fumble through their pockets,
for a last token of endurance,
one fragment of compassion
Blind photographers record
plagiarism of crows,
re-enactments of a mystery
surrendering to itself

Metaphysical castle walls
indestructibly corrode
Snake oil salesmen wait
dispassionately to be desired
From a great and final sleep
nocturnal loves ascend
Tricksters and magicians
have nothing left to nurture

An old fool in the park
talks philosophy of elms,
how flowers circumvent
their moment of conception
A woman in white beside him,
her head in gold memoriam,

consults her grip in time,
to strings of tinkling cymbals
 Ignoring blue impressions

that all consists of waves,
staring into wickedness,
they treat their bereavements
as an emperor would a vagrant
A city behind them perishes,
not like Sodom or Gomorrah,
more the heart of Oceania

This is not the day of wrath
or meekness or contrition
Each move simultaneously
enslaves us & unchains us
We dream that we are dreaming
but God shall wake to God
The chronometer is stopped
by precise yet tender hands

A STRATEGY OF MIRRORS

FRACTALS OF THE CATHKIN BRAES

Tragically persistent, a work of beauty
flawed on purpose, city views subscribe
to bastardisation, space, time
and devious rhyme
Neither victim nor perpetrator,
dark is sweet, light grows bitter,
nothing else needs reversed,
before iron ravens, sparrows of steel,
no vision of ice diminished by heat,

traffic moves
unperturbed by distance,
commuters forget
what they've learned of death,
be a moon in water or a sea on fire,
metal faces of leviathans
become like milk,
ripple, curdle, towards their margins
Machines shall thrive alive in deadness,
the dead only speak to the dead,
this is why we envy them

Sometimes there are no other
shapes but circles, when within them
we recall who we are. Glasgow a book
with torn out pages
fluttering in purgatorial wind,
half-words and letters floating, dancing,

a flotilla of eyes unable
to transmit or receive,
self-containing
to point of implosion, craving

gourmet oblivion
Fractals of the Cathkin Braes
seek to signal their own
narcoleptic shadows, sheets where ghosts
have no other option
but to choose to remain there
No word once written erased completely,
a law no human hand could enforce,

linger architectural
transcriptions of a universe
whose planets only appear to collide,
but in fact, move through each other
like water moves through water
Artifice concedes to artifice,
flesh concedes to flesh,
the electric becomes electric

DEREK J BROWN

A STRATEGY OF MIRRORS

TWO LOVERS LOST IN A TRAIN COMPARTMENT

Address the dark dream, its obsidian bubbles,
the presence of backrooms in Heaven,
wind turbines on the oblivious hill
in their constant operation
offer us no hints
as to minerals of mysteries,
sensations of a shift
in what is more than time or space,
illusions of bridges and creeks,
representatives of glass,

flirtations with orange balls on sandless beaches,
debates on the colours of leaves,
or when hate conceals its features,
or if winter is really spring,
or if spring is really autumn

CITY FRAGMENT THRU A FRACTURED LENS

DEREK J BROWN

I

Tinselled nebulae scatter, we dance a dance of meridians,
seekers of that dream we do not seek, we
sense everything to come already is antique, that tragic
is everything. Reverent this aloneness,

giving a hand to cantatas on fringes of warped antennas,
cadences of sad prosperity, we watch the whites congeal,
the blacks as they run down crumbling palisades
This day shall not divulge its affinity with night,

only scars of a majesty it knows will fade
Near dressing room windows of tragediennes, we stop,
below unearthly hints, lenticular skylights,
ghosts of flying saucers, we must look to ourselves,

as we, ourselves. Lapis supplications of beggars
linger like the sun's imprint on the retina, music's vacuum
music also as we enter the gates of Kelvingrove Park,
thru warm winter cylinders that are summer's spectres,

covert stagnancies, simulations of belonging
The bandstand now a threshold for outlaws long extinct,
sequined magi pour on surfaces mutations of a style,
and the damaged damaged more by hands that must repair
and (not like sparrows) drop the masses dumb
  commemorations
No souls tortured here, only teased,

A STRATEGY OF MIRRORS

as denizens of this black tooth town careen towards their
   goals,
like paths of prisms towards supernovas

II

Do you pity them? Do you pity us? We who always see
shadows behind us in every mirror, we curse you sometimes,
when memory moves into its stillness,
when memory has a memory that is only of itself

Passing See Saw Marjorie Daws,
midnight matinees, corkscrew merry-go-rounds,
cruel ejaculations of this Cimmerian Glasgow day
You, inventor of all shape and shapelessness, taunt us now as
always,

in voluptuousness of a sphere struck more present by its
   absence,
stock-still violations of time that envies space
Should we in you
believe? From the fear of not believing?
Is the answer in this question?

Or in the wannabe Hopper cafés where white widows sip
   black tea?
In Dali's St John of the Cross? In some readymade by
   Duchamp?
I suppose we'll just keep looking, all the while pretending
   not to,
go sit beneath white buildings, towers with sea-blue broken
   clocks

III

The Giaconda smiles of the women circulate like arctic
  storms,
tease harmless minds that wander museums inside museums
Magicians always seem to use such ordinary objects,
just like holy fools, godless angels, have we always been so
  blind

to temperature inversions, fraudulent horizons,
we who are the authors of a science estranged from science,
whose principles of pleasure go beyond sensation's strings
No bridge that goes to nowhere is a bridge that we would
  cross

Instead we walk so slowly through palaces stripped of
  curtains,
tracing our lost steps across ebb of stone and glass,
armed with phantom explanations and husks of crooked
  souls,
while evening's signs go tumbling down Jack and Jill do
  mains

So, rouse your reckless sleepers now, like long forgotten
  statues
we see ourselves begin to crumble, LORD, return us now
  to us,
thru the final before and after, cruel ellipse and circuit sense,
malicious hands, corrupted eyes, and thru one fractured lens!

STATUE OF AN ARMLESS WOMAN

It feels like I'm almost
in love with the statue of an armless woman
So white, so much whiter than white,
so white it makes you wish you were blind,
makes you feel like gnawing the rind
off a blood red orange

In the town square near the fountain
is the statue of an armless woman,
so becoming, so becoming that it makes you feel
like you haven't yet begun,
and you're envious of lovers jaundiced
in the late June sun

The moon moth absorbs its light, is grateful for it
yet does not bask too much
in the ever so slow
tossing off of loneliness,
the deep silence
of a shallow mirror, a death that is not death
Come over to the other side,
see infernal circles
above chairs and tables
of a Mediterranean cafe

I have never known such a heat
to cancel itself out,
in the not so distant distance

my eyes ingest the image
of the statue of an armless woman

There's the interminable ring of a telephone
and a place I cannot find
An undefined thing frustrates,
gnaws and repeats
Hieroglyphs everywhere,
high above my head, underneath my feet

There's a convulsing of limbs,
a battle of hers and hims,
jargon of a million dreamers
and the statue of an armless woman,

a death that hides its privilege,
a life that has no end, an intermingling
of those that know in advance
the answers to their questions
All around,
children ask what the grass is,
they know what the grass is,
they just pretend not to
Beyond this phase of neither
remains the statue of an armless woman

There are young men revelling
in cruelties of roses, in time's brilliant paleness
There are laughing clowns laughing
at laughing clowns,

A STRATEGY OF MIRRORS

a constant amassing of mouths
whose words I pray demean,
and the eyes, the eyes of a statue,
the statue of an armless woman

ONE MAN CAUGHT IN A MULTITUDE OF SELF

DEREK J BROWN

Outside a crowded cafe, at a solitary table, on a solitary chair
sits a solitary man, his every thought once thought before,
by another version of himself, a twentieth century duplicate,
or maybe a nineteenth, or even going all the way back
to invention of beginning

From his hometown main street, what is present, he
    considers,
a possibility, a time in which the guilt was not so much,
sees tenements that once were there, strange hybrids
of old and new, a church made into a temple of state
(although church was always church and state was always
    state)

open-air rooftop ballrooms, women in satin gowns,
men in silk tuxedos, muses caught in razor wire,
green screen polymorphs, stop-motion cabarets,
funhouse glass reflections, midnight insurrections,
aftermaths of tunnels, half-constructed bridges,

cosmogonic life-reviews, toy soldiers marching
thru claret painted dawns, paralytic ballet dancers
cursing autumn moonlight, arcades where things are sold,
not bought, crumbling balconies from where
one might see there is something more than distance

An idea anything is possible in the moment that it isn't
runs throughout his Isness, as he wanders by the bandstand

where dead men once played, where leaves now fall,
the park with all its tones of a counterfeit aloneness
oozing metaphor for a place outside oblivion,

not so much a shelter than a space for recognition
Descendants on the streets of their descendants
continue still the certainty they are all that ever live,
continue still, these people among insects of their time,
orphans born subservient to a covert undulation,

physical apparitions consult November's moon,
basement level dwellers fight by proxy for the state
while others wait for justice, the kind that comes too late
A watchman for an instance, thru a reverence of veils,
a stratagem of eyes, surveilled as he surveils,

cars pass; no one seems within them,
from sides of buses beam diaphanous subliminals,
tinsel portents in reverse, the town clock tells a time
where nothing is male or female,
a multiplicity dictates, condemning grandfathers

for having once obeyed, it still demands submission
Around him spreads a sound of industry and trade,
of equality and nakedness, it is in fact
a silence barely broken by an apostasy of sighs,
a silence that appears to ask a question,

the answer itself the question, a question like no other
One man caught in a multitude of self,

one man caught beside himself,
his eye swearing to see beyond the sandstone vistas,
beyond the graves where pacts were signed,

beyond precious bric-a-brac, beyond ancient doorways
where Antonios deal with Shylocks,
beyond markets where the key is cheapness,
beyond fountains inscribed with names of queens,
beyond dogs that walk their owners,

beyond pageantry of pigeons
The permanence of change upsets him,
sets him up in moments in which things remain the same,
a voice says everything that should be brief
is brief, lies and speaks of itself; speaks of itself and lies

beyond the dogs that walk their owners,
beyond the pageantry of pigeons
The permanence of change upsets him,
it sets him up in moments in which things remain the same
A voice says everything that should be brief is brief,
it speaks of itself and it lies

DEREK J BROWN

ASHTRAY BLUES

O most disconsolate ashtray, you are not politically correct,
it's a conspiracy I suspect

O most disconsolate ashtray, how I long
to see your smoke arise, suspended in my eyes,
now you have nothing left to do
but linger in a smokeless state,
an archaic paperweight,

sun persecuting
where there was once a wealth of ash
O inanimate one, am I somehow inanimate too?
An emptiness incarnate? A renegade shade of blue?
O most disconsolate ashtray, it's such a shame
you're obsolete

O how I hate to see you sweating in the heat! So tragic, so
  conspicuous

But you're not alone, I'm alone too,
a broke-down engine, a holographic Christ,
a cucumber sandwich, a sculpture made of ice,
an analogue TV,
a thing of darkest matter, a thing no eye can see
I'm a postcard from a railway station no longer in existence,
a letter from someone no longer alive
to someone no longer alive,
an ant without a colony, a bee without a hive,

something watered down, something disinfected,
a nonsensical list of things completely unconnected

Can you recognize eternity? Heresy bon vivant? Anarchy
  demure?
Do you see it there? (corresponding casually with earth and
  moon)
a sun far too resplendent, too childish, too jejune

O most disconsolate ashtray made of finest glass,
do you see those philistines as they pass?
In monstrous motor cars, cold steel Goliaths
Do you see their grand hypocrisies?

I was that laughing clown
in the store-front window, the one that laughed an age ago,
the one that laughs no more

I was that proud misfit,
arms folded like an Indian, dreaming of meridian
I was that undertaker who misplaced his make-up case,
a cartoon born philosopher of no real time or place

And if there really is such a thing as reincarnation,
I would be proud to be an ashtray

ST ANDREW'S BRIDGE

This is the season of swords and insects
No mirror defines, no man reflects
Hylas and the nymphs together recline
in a desolate rapture, deprived of their wine

Ravens cease talking and inspect sacrament
Metallic air flows with unyielding intent
Thru houses rich with vermin, thru vein and artery
Serpentine streets, malign municipality

No time for sentiment, or neon marionette
Lovers still seek fruit, consult moons that don't set
Beneath erratic metronomes, auroral civic light
Divergent shadows greet each pseudoparasite

Factory ghosts, although hidden still haunt
Pass judges of hope, wardens of want
Fountains spout liquid, proposing a dream
That each mind adapts to its own cruel regime

St Andrew's Bridge looms, Glasgow Green sleeps
With/without shepherd sheep remain sheep
The legend of Catherine still pulses, radiates
None weep with pity, righteousness waits

Professional victims, a theatrical crew
Bodies outlined in yellow and blue
Squeal like pigs, bark like baboons
Tend to their own immaculate wounds

Soothsayers harness an illusory flame
On cunei clay tablets inscribe a false name
Church gables crumble, crosses invert
Agents of famine await their dessert

Tamed birds of prey, prettified, preened
Squirm and recoil from a fictional fiend
Unnamed characters from a sci-fi novel
Nullify, invent, prostrate and grovel

Patiently wait for the next crucial scene
Flesh and blood cogs in an abstract machine
Nelson's monument stands, a tall yet frail guard
Guards against what? The invisible, unscarred

Quiet, indeterminate, wraiths of contention
McLennan Arch an image for another dimension
Upon the grey River Clyde swans appear black
And still maintain grace whatever they lack

Tonight's moon illumines a conflict of mass
The stained yet aqueous pavilion of glass
A thousand souls cross St Andrew's Bridge
Subjects no longer of grand sacrilege

A mother and daughter, break, scatter bread
Stand still like ravens awaiting their dead
No mirror defines and no one reflects
This is the season of swords and insects

TEN SWORDS

A dream reconstructed, monument to
the incomplete, shape impossible
to determine. Speak for yourself,
you don't have a tongue? So be it

I can't bring myself to worship you
You bid me explain, I don't need to explain,
I won't explain. Woke up this morning,
ten swords on my back, that I couldn't feel

or see, except for drops of blood
on white linen. Gone for now, they might return,
Jungian entities, existential spectres,
atmospheric blasts from a Jovian dimension

A darkness we sense is our own transmits,
nourishes, keeps us alive for cryptic reasons,
like strange music from a star that vibrates
defying repeatedly interpretation

Some protect the sparrows from the crows,
some sneer at nature, at the subtle act of falling,
dormant expressions of the desire to be home
If I must confess

I must confess, it will not be to you
what it is to me, the bluest truths,
the reddest myths, navigate the cosmic mists
No more seeking simplicity, in the pulpous eye

of solidity, no more giving of keys to keep,
no more dreaming, a depleted sleep,
no more kneeling to kiss the ground, no more lost,
no more unbound, only a circle, memory,

sound. Do I speak like a man who's been burned?
A man whose eyes have slowly turned,
to the moon's obscure
humility

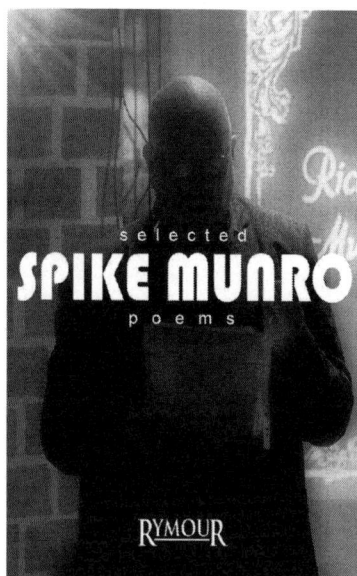

selected
SPIKE MUNRO
poems

RYMOUR

Munro's poetry reveals a delightful rapier wit, slashing at political, environmental and cultural orthodoxies, jabbing at the absurdity of everyday life.

ASIF KHAN

RYMOUR BOOKS

POETRY • PROSE • DEBATE